INTRODUCTION

TO

GEOGRAPHY

WRITTEN BY: Frank Philemon
P.O. Box, 116,
LIWALE-LINDI
TANZANIA
+255762426746
naxfra@gmail.com
© 2017

CONTENTS

ACKNOWLEDGEMENT

This book is a result of the effort and contribution of many people in which I sincerely acknowledge them in supporting directly or indirectly the work of this book. I thank a lot the members of academic staff especially the department of geography at Liwale high school for their challenging ideas that developed this book.

I also extend my gratitude to the Heavenly Almighty God for His protection and blessings to my life. Other special thanks I extend to my lovely wife, Mariam Lucas and beloved son, Kevin Frank as well as Naxfra Mixed Education Enrichment (N.M.E.E) for extending their hearts and hands so as to cooperate with me in accomplishing the work of this book.

Amazon Company is the last but the least. Thank you for sacrificing your comfort and rights the greater good. God bless you all the individuals who have in their personal and official capacity, contributed in one way or another for realization of this book are sincerely acknowledge; without your effort this book would not be accomplished.

Frank Philemon
naxfra@gmail.com
© 2017

PREFACE

Introduction to Geography is the book developed through maximization of simplification of basic concepts about geography. This makes its content easily accessible to all geographers and students in primary level, ordinary level, advanced level high and college education.

This book has been written with the strong aim of helping geographers and alike in getting in-depth understanding and improving their knowledge and skills in all issues of geography. The author is confident that this book will be an invaluable asset for primary schools, secondary schools and colleges, and that students as well as teachers will find it useful in making the teaching and learning process easier, pleasant and more fruitful.

Any efforts and contribution in one way or another incurred by all people so as to accomplish the work of this book is acknowledged; without their support this book would not have been written and seen by all of the people of the earth planet. I acknowledge all writers that I used their books as references to complete the work of this book.

Frank Philemon
naxfra@gmail.com
© 2017

DEDICATION

This book I dedicate to my beloved son; **Kevin Frank** in bringing happiness to my life. From him, people are calling me a father.

CHAPTER ONE

THE CONCEPT OF GEOGRAPHY

Definition of Geography

Geography as the field of study can be defined in a different ways. Some of the Geography definitions are: Geography is the scientific study of man's life in relation to the environment. Geography is the study of the systems and processes involved in the world's weather, mountains, seas, lakes etc. and of the ways in which countries and people organize life within an area. Geography is also defined as the study of spatial distribution of physical and cultural features of landscape and biosphere in relation to the races of mankind. Geography also can be defined as the scientific study of the earth as a home to humankind.

The Origin or Etymology of the Word Geography

The word *"geography"* was first used by a Greek mathematician, geographer, poet, astronomer and music theorist called *Eratosthenes*. The word geography is the combination of two Greek words, *'Geo'* and *'Graphein' (or grapho)*. **Geo** means "the Earth" and **Graphein** mean "to write", "to draw" or "to describe". These two words together formed **Geographia**, which means *to draw, to write about or describe the Earth*. These meanings led to the development of the early definition of Geography which referred to description of the Earth by words, maps and statistics including both the physical earth and everything found on it such as plants, animals and people.

Therefore; Geography is the study of the distribution and interrelationship of phenomena in relation to earth's surface or Geography is the study of the Earth and its environment. Something to note is that; geography has relationship between environment and humankind. The word environment can be defined as all things that surround human being. Cultural environment is the link between man and surroundings. In the study of geography, there are two categories of environment:

Physical environment: This refers to all natural physical features on the earth, such as land, water, climate, plant, animals and human being.

Human environment: This refers to the environment in relation to human kind's activities, like farming, mining, settlement, tourism and other related human activities.

Branches of Geography

There are three main branches of Geography, namely:

1. Physical Geography. This is the branch of geography that deals with the study of natural physical environment; which is mainly concerned with land formation processes, weather and climate, solar systems, soil and rocks, animal and vegetation or plants.

2. **Human and Economic Geography**. This branch of geography involves the study of human and their activities on the Earth's surface. The branch includes the study of human settlements, human population, and all human activities undertaken by mankind.

3. Practical Geography. It is the branch of geography that deals with practical skills of both human and physical geography, which is concerned with field study of photography, map interpretation, application of statistics, research and survey.

Importance of Studying Geography

There are thousands importance of geography but some few significances can be outlined. We study Geography in order to:

1. Raise our standard of living by utilizing properly the available resources.
2. Understand the social and geographical problems and how to solve them. For example soil erosion, climate problems etc.

3. Gain skills of observation, measuring, recording and interpreting of phenomena.
4. Expand our knowledge of employment opportunities through specialized field.
5. Acquire skills for combating environmental problems such as drought, global warming etc.
6. Understand the interactions between our country and other countries and share ideas of solving problems.
7. Understand how landforms are formed.
8. Enable people to appreciate nature.
9. Be aware with our country and our heritage.

Relationship of Geography with Other Field of Studies or Disciplines

Geography occupies the central position in the sphere of all the physical and human environmental science. Geography is a multidimensional subject applying well defined methods of studying it. Geography is regarded or considered as a human science but also a physical science.

By definition, *field of study* refers to the knowledge of a particular area or subject. Field of study means the subject. *Geographical phenomena* refer to the geographical facts or events of scientific interest. Interrelated geographical phenomena are:

a) Land provides soil in which plants grow. Plants are food for herbivores that turns to be food for carnivores and humankind.

b) Climate determines the types of plant and animal those can survive in a given region. Climate determines the activities of people and distribution of population.

Interrelationship between geography and other field of study (subjects) involves the study of geography in relation to others subjects. Geography is a very broad field of inquiry and "borrows" its object of study from the entire following related field of studies:

Mathematics: Geography tends to deploy and use mathematical calculation to calculate distance, area, scale, bearing etc.

Physics: As in physics, also geography deals with matter, energy, forces and gravitation.

History: Geography attempt to explain where events, landforms, took place. Geography itself has an origin (history) in its evolution and development. The study of history in geography is represented by *Geological Time Scale.*

Biology: Geography facts and focuses on plants and animals as biology concerns. *Biography* involves both botany and zoology.

Chemistry: In geography there is the study of chemical reaction especially in chemical weathering process, in soil formation process and formation of features in karst region (limestone areas) there should be the chemical reaction. The study chemistry in geography called *Geochemistry.*

Civics: Political boundaries and political interactions among the people of different country as in civics also can be described in geography through human geography, statistical geography and geographical maps. *Political Geography* (from Political Science) both concerned with the comparative study of different governments and international relations.

Geomorphology (from geology): The interpretative description of the landforms or relief features of the Earth's surface. Therefore, see the table that shows about interrelation of Geography:

	Field of study/subject	*Interrelation*
	Biology	Biogeography
	Physics	Geophysics
Geography	Mathematics	Practical geography
	Botany	Plant geography
	Zoology	Zoogeography
	Geology	Geomorphology
	History	Geological time scale

Other Fields of Studies (Subjects) that Interrelate with Geography are:
Paleontology: It is the study of fossils. In the study of rocks, most of sedimentary rocks comprise fossil materials.

Ecology (environment with organisms): The study of the interrelationship of organisms and their environment.

Zoogeography (from Zoology): Concerned with the distribution of animals and with their adaptations, or their restriction by environment.

Phytogeography (from Botany): the science that deals with plants' life, structure and growth.

Pedageography (from Pedology): Concerned with the distribution of soils.

Evolution of Geography Thoughts

Evolution means changes that have taken place. Evolution of geography is the changes that taken place in geography. At the beginning geography started as a simple description and it is evolved up to complex discipline or phenomena. Changes in geography are challenges faced geography as a discipline.

Geography like any other discipline, faced with problems in organizing materials and approaches. Geography undergone the following different (six) phases or evolution so as to be described as a discipline:

1. *Exploration Phase*

At this period there was industrial countries were exploring new lands in the 15th Century. Therefore, geography at this time people concerned where the materials are found, hence by that time geography was taught in order to know and collect information in different phenomena and where materials (like minerals) are found and geography was based to find the location of the materials where are found. Interest of the people were taught through description, simply to describe the phenomena as existed as well as students of geography were only required to know the inventory of things and place naming e.g. who is discovered and where it found.

The weakness of this phase (approach or theory) is that, failed to explain for the occurrence of the phenomena (on how the phenomena was found) and there were no chance to question about. This phase was abandoned following to another phase so as to collect its weakness.

2. *Environmental Determinism Phase*

This phase was influenced by *Charles Darwin*. Physical environment controlled this phase because it controlled what people did in that particular period. Under this paradigm there was a belief that, nature of human activity was controlled by the physical environment and that man is a product of the earth's surface. At time went on, geographers started to question about this phase e.g. why mineral is found here and not in other place in this region.

Geographical teaching at this phase or period was mainly influenced with physical environment on man or human activities and physical environment was a determinant factor. Geography moved from description to explanation. Example, why this phenomena is found here and not there? Weakness of this paradigm: in reality not all physical environment can determine human activities even though it is a determinant factor.

3. *Regionalism Phase*

This phase dominated geographical thinking before the 2nd world war. The interest of geographers was to attack or oppose the environmentalism approach. It concerned with identification of uniqueness of the regions; as said that, in each region man and nature were seemed to adopt each other. (Meaning that, you cannot distinguish nature and man.

Geography was taught through how to distinguish about how region differ from one to another. The students of geography knew the different between one region and location to another. Weakness of this paradigm: thinkers of this phase said that geography lacked theory to guide different regions. This phase it also rooted in environmental determinism i.e. physical environment is a determinant factor.

4. Quantitative Revolution Phase

This phase came to fill the gap of regional approach that lacked theories. It came with different ideas in order to shape the discipline. In this phase geographers started to make laws or theories so as to criticize the previous. Advocators of this phase, said geography were a spatial science and geometry was the language for the analysis of spatial form. They thought that it is important to formulate laws or theories on the cause and effect relationship, hence lead to the introduction of geometry, practical geography in this discipline.

Geography in this phase started to be accurate, specific, and strict because people followed laws and theories. Even though somehow the phase was so much good, but there were some challenges like: it placed too much emphasis on making and testing theories and paid more explanation to the phenomena. It involved too much mathematical calculation (geometry). Put behind behavior as a determinant factor.

5. Behaviorism Phase

For behaviorism argument is that, laws or theories are insignificant (not enough) for understanding how those pertaining come to being. In this phase, it advocated that behavior plays an important role in understanding of the spatial distribution and patterns of manmade phenomena on the earth's surface. Weakness: behaviorists they didn't give critical view of the spatial inequalities.

6. Radicalism Phase

The radical approach to geography it rose in 1970 to add a new dimension in geography discipline. Radicalism presented a critical view of spatial inequalities which the previous phase failed to do this. Influenced by *Marxist theory* and in this phase, the main emphasis is, the differences in physical environmental factors and the behavior of the individual are not sufficient to the spatial variation of phenomena. They said, there other factors which can determine the spatial phenomena like organization of the society, political structure and alike.

TRIAL QUESTIONS:

1. Define and write short notes about the following terms:
   a) Environment
   b) Geography

2. What does it mean of the following words:
   a) Geo
   b) Graphien or grapho

3. List down six importance of studying geography.

4. Identify the branches of geography, and explain about what each deals with?

5. List seven jobs one can do using the knowledge acquired from studying geography.

6. Discuss the evolution of geography and challenges or weakness from each phase.

CHAPTER TWO

THE MAJOR FEATURES OF THE EARTH'S SURFACE

The surface of the earth is made up of two main features: *1. Land and 2. Water bodies.* The land surface is estimated at **29.2%** of the total area of the earth's surface while water covers the remaining **70.2%**. The most of the land exists in large block called **continents**; likewise, the most of the water is contained in large water bodies called **seas** and **oceans**.

Definitions of Some Terms:

Canal is the small mass of land joining two continents. (e.g. sues canal). **Gulf** is the water inlet to the land (e.g. gulf of guinea, Mexico and Banguela). **Strait** is the narrow water path that separates one land mass from another (e.g. Gibraltar in morocco, Makasan in Indonesia). **Peninsula** is a part of land entering in a body of water (e.g. Msasani in Tanzania and Indian peninsula). **Cape** is piece of land getting in the sea (e.g. Cape of Good Hope in South Africa, Cape Verde, and Palmas).

A. CONTINENTS

By definition, **continent** refers to a major landmass rising from the ocean floor. Continent is surrounded by water bodies. Continents rise from ocean floors. There are seven continents on the earth's surface. These are:

1) Africa
2) Asia
3) Australia
4) Europe
5) Antarctica
6) South America
7) North America

Most of the continents are joined together by small mass of land, like Suez Canal, that connects Africa and Asia, Panama Isthmus join North America and South America. The Northern hemisphere is covered by more land surface whereas southern hemisphere occupies small part of it.

All continents originated from the drifting apart of one *Sialic* known as *Pangaea* over million years ago. See the figure below:

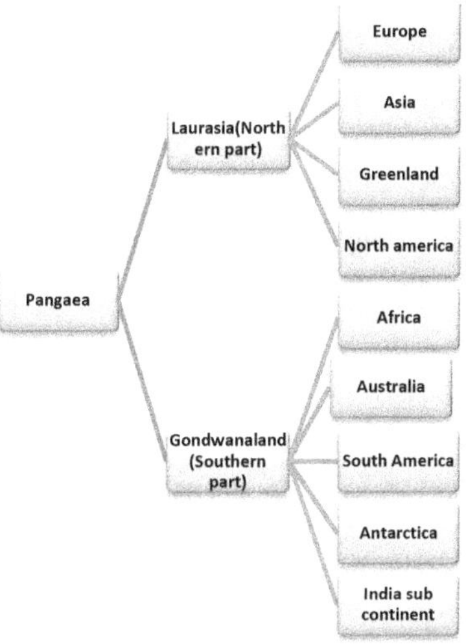

Asia

Asia is the largest continent in the world covering more than one third of the earth's surface. The continent has total areas of 43.6 million kilometer square and lies from 0^0 to 67^0N and 30^0E about 180^0E.

Africa

Africa is the second largest continent in the world, covers 30.3 million km². It Lies from 35^0N and 37^0N to 160^0W.

North America

It is the third largest continent, which covers 25.3 Million Km². It extends from 10⁰N to 65⁰N and from 60⁰W to 160⁰W.

South America:

It is the fourth largest continent that covers about 17.6 million kilometer square extending from 10⁰N and 50⁰S and between 35⁰W and 80⁰W.

Antarctica

It lies within latitude 66⁰S covering the area of about 13.3 million km². Antarctica is the fifth largest continent in size and therefore it is the only the uninhibited continent.

Europe

Europe is the sixth largest continent in size that separated from Asia by Ural Mountain to East side. Its total area is about 10.5 million kilometer square.

Australia

It is the smallest continent in size. Its total area is about 7.7 million kilometer square. The following table shows the size of continents:

Continent	Area (Km2)
Asia	43, 608, 000
Africa	30, 335, 000
North America	25, 349, 000
South America	17, 611, 000
Antarctica	13, 340, 000
Europe	10, 498, 000
Australia	7, 682, 000

The following map shows the distribution of Continents on the Earth's surface:

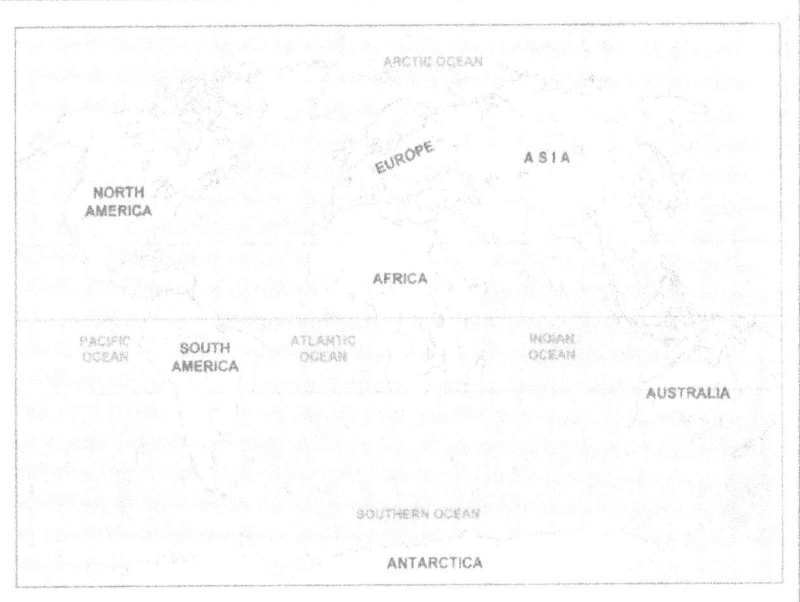

The Major Feature of the Continents:

The surface of any continent is not smooth due to the agents of denudation and deposition. Features (relief features) are hills, mountains, rift valley, plains, plateaus and basins. Mountains, plains and plateaus forms the major relief features of the continents.

1. *Plains*

Plain is an undulating land usually near to the sea level. Plains are large and nearly flat stretch of land that usually has no great change in its height. Plains are characterized by very gentle slopes and wide valleys. Such plain are described as *rolling* or *undulating* plains and Serengeti Plain is an example of such plain that found in Tanzania. Many plains are found in coastal areas of the continents, which are called *coastal plains.* Many of plains are caused by down warping of the earth's crust. North Europe plain, Siberia plain, and the great central pain of America are example of the plain.

2. Plateaus

Plateaus are extensive high altitude areas with more or less uniform summit levels. Plateaus are described as *table-lands.* Most of plateaus are resulted due to the warping of the earth's crust that caused by uplifting of some areas. Plateaus that are covered by thick layers of volcanic lava are called *lava-plateaus.* Brasilia highland, central plateau of Africa, Colombia plateau, Decan plateau of India and Ethiopian plateau are examples of the plateaus.

3. Mountains

Mountain is the highland areas rising above mean sea level. There are various types of mountains formed depending to their mode of formation. There are major four types of mountains that named according to their mode of formation:

- a) Fold Mountains
- b) Block Mountains
- c) Volcanic Mountains
- d) Residual Mountains

(a) Volcanic Mountains

Volcanic mountains are mountains formed from the pilling up and cooling of molten lava and ashes that are thrown out from the earth's interior after volcanic eruption. Most of the volcanic mountains contains craters at their peaks and are conical in shape. Crater can be filled with water to form lake like Ngorongoro in Arusha. There are major three classifications of volcanic mountains:

1. *Active volcanoes:* are volcanic mountains which still experiencing periodic

eruptions and erupted in the recent periods. Mount Vesuvius and Stromboli in Italy, mount Mauna Loa in Hawaii, Krakatau in Indonesia, Mufumbiro in Uganda, Oldonyolengai in Tanzania are examples of active volcanoes.

2. *Dormant volcanoes:* are those mountains which have erupted once in the past but have remained inactive for fairly long period. These are called *sleeping* volcanoes which become active once again. Examples of dormant volcanoes are Kilimanjaro Mountain and Meru Mountain in Tanzania.

Mount Kilimanjalo in Tanzania

3. *Extinct (dead) volcanoes:* are those mountains which were active but not erupted for a very long time and have not shown any sign of erupting again. Elgon, Ngorongoro, Kenya and Rungwe in East Africa are examples of dead volcanoes.

(b) Fold Mountains

Fold Mountains are formed by wrinkling of the earth's crust caused by compressional forces. In them, they occur when sedimentary rocks are laid in horizontal layers which were later folded by compressional forces. Most of the ranges in the world are formed by fold Mountains, like cape ranges in South Africa, Mount Everest of Himalaya, Atlas, Alps, Appalachians in U.S.A and the great divided ranges of Australia. The *anticline* is the *up fold* and *syncline* is the *down fold* of the fold mountain.

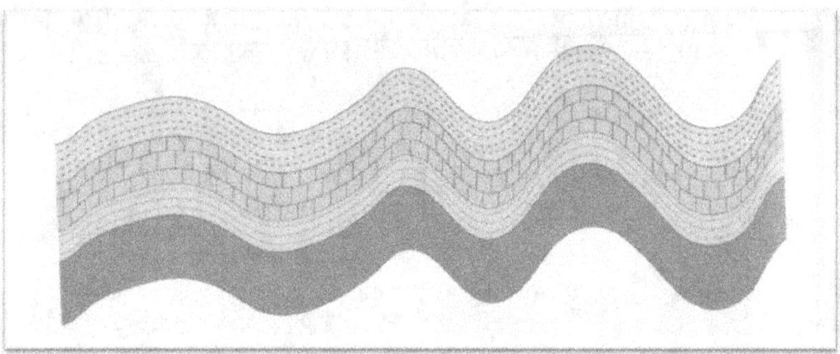

(c) Block Mountains (Horst)

Block Mountain is an upland bordered by faults on one or more sides. Block Mountain formed due to being raised or tilted up by the earth movement along faults bounded block. Block Mountain does not cover large area like fold mountain. Examples of Block Mountain are mountain Sinai in Asia, Ruwenzori in Tanzania. Block Mountains are associated with rift valleys.

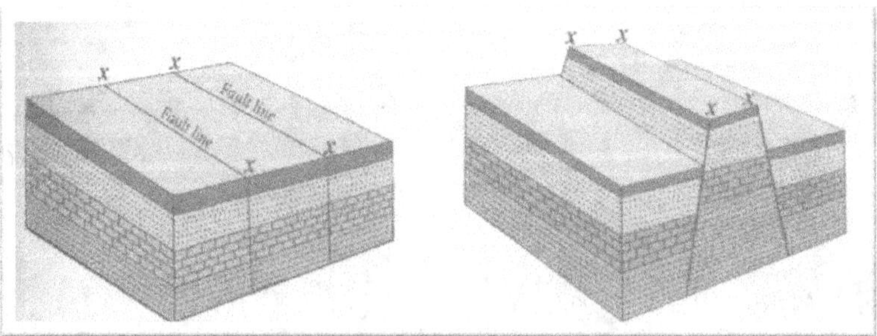

(d) Residual Mountains

Residual mountains are formed by prolonged denudations. Sekenke hills in Singida Tanzania, Mesas and Buttes in US and Adamawa in Nigeria.

4 Rift Valleys (Grabens)

Rift valley is an elongated trough or depression formed when two sets of faults sink down. The Great East African rift valley is an example. Sometimes trenches are filled with water to form lakes. The bottom of a valley is called is called *floor* and valley's side are called *valley-walls* or *valley-slopes*.

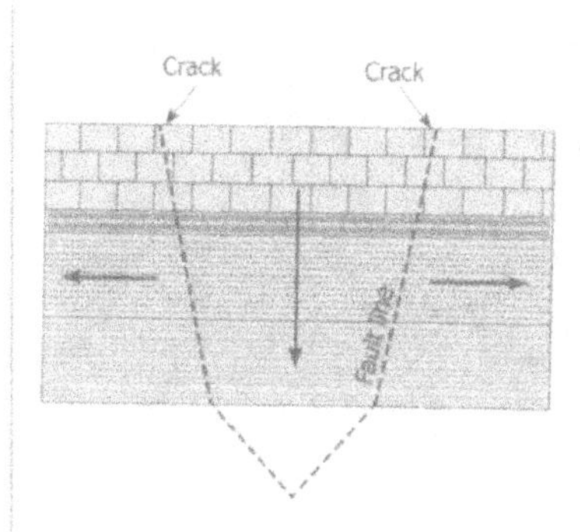

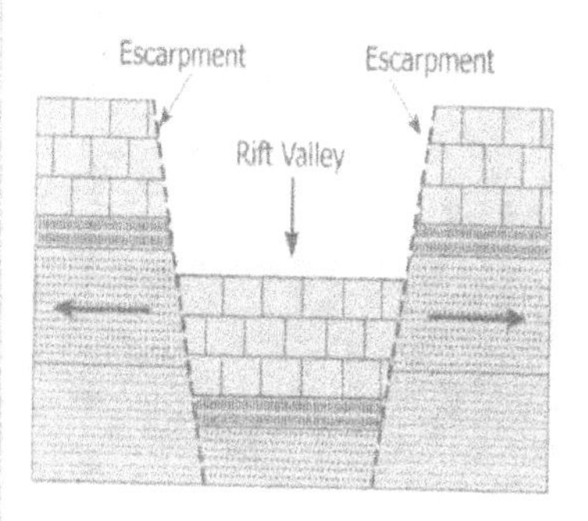

5 Basins

Basin is the natural or artificial depression varying in size on the Earth's surface. If basins are filled with or occupied by water, tend to form rivers or lakes and ocean basin. Examples of basins are Lake Victoria, Congo basin, Kalahari basin, Chad and Sudan basin.

6 Drainages

Drainage refers to the situation by which, water are removed from an area. Streams and rivers are responsible for draining the land surfaces. The processes of water to flow on the ground are known as overland flow, and if water percolates into the ground are called *underground water.* Surface flow of water from rainfall or snow-melt over the ground is known as *water runoff.*

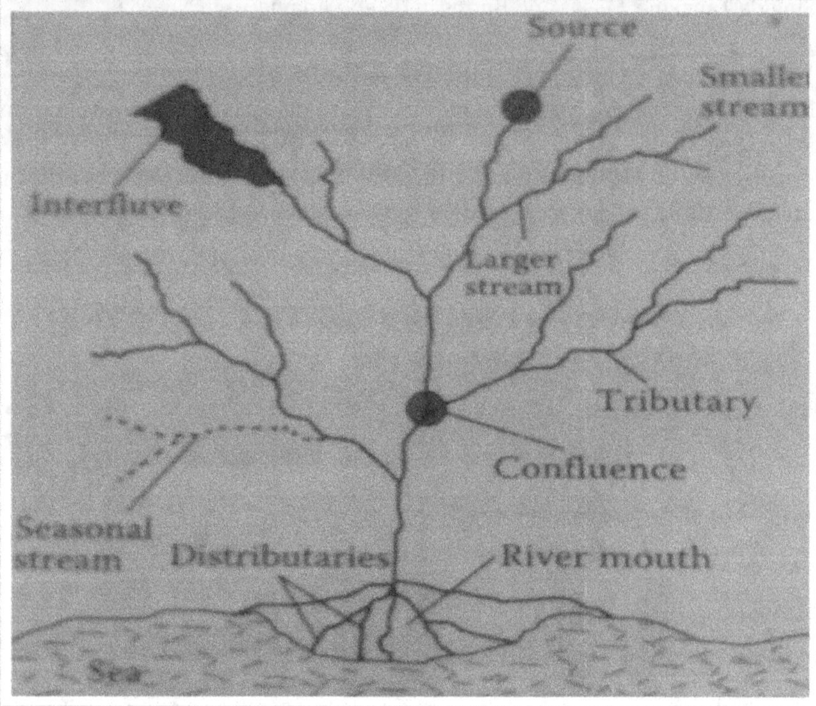

The surface water from rainfall or snow-melt flows in small channels, which finally join to form large trenches of rivers are called *tributaries.* Small streams that branches off before they enter the sea or lake are known as *distributaries.* The area from which a river system collects its rain water is called *river/basin/catchment area/drainage basin.* The boundary between one catchment area and the next is formed by crest line of the surrounding highland called *watershed/water divide/basin perimeter* and the main river and its tributaries together forms *river system.*

B. WATER BODIES

Water body is any significant accumulation of water such as ocean, lake, river and other alike. Some water bodies are manmade (artificial). Navigable water bodies are called *water ways*. There are more water bodies in the southern hemisphere than the northern hemisphere.

1. Oceans

Ocean is a large body of water that surrounds the landmasses of the earth. Ocean covers almost 360 million kilometer square which is equal to 71%. The Pacific Ocean is the ocean while Arctic Ocean is the smallest ocean.

Salinity of ocean water depends on the temperature, amount of fresh water entering in the ocean, nature of the rock of the ocean floor and additional of organic materials. The following is the table that shows the five large oceans in the world:

Ocean	Area (Km^2)	Average Depth (M)
Pacific	155, 557, 000	4, 028
Atlantic	76, 762, 000	3, 926
Indian	68, 556, 000	3, 936
Southern	20, 327, 000	4, 000 to 5, 000
Arctic	14, 056, 000	1, 205

Types of Water Movement In oceans

Water moves in the oceans is into two main ways:
   a) *Horizontal movement:* e.g. tides and currents.
   b) *Vertical movement:* e.g. Sinking and rising of water.

Ocean currents: Ocean current is the movement of surface water. There are two types of ocean currents: *Warm ocean currents*: these are ocean currents formed by masses of warm water e.g. Mozambique, Brazilia ocean currents. And the second is *cold* or *cool ocean currents*: these are ocean currents that formed by masses of cold water e.g. California, Benguela, and West Australia ocean currents.

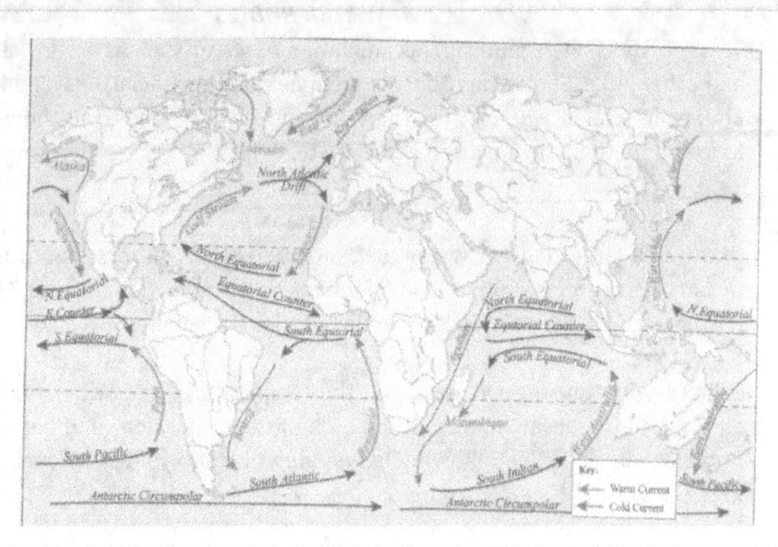

Tides: Tides are periodic rise and fall in the level of water in the oceans and sea. Tides occur twice a day (in 24 hours). Tides are caused by the sun and to a greater exert the moon exerts a gravitational attraction on the earth's surface.

Waves: Waves are the up and down movements of the surface water. There are two parts of lakes, sea and ocean waves: *Trough:* is the lowest part of the wave and *Crest:* is the highest part of the wave.

The distance between one crest to another is called *wavelength*. Waves are caused by winds which drive them to the shore. Wave travel in a defined direction, whereas water moves up and down.

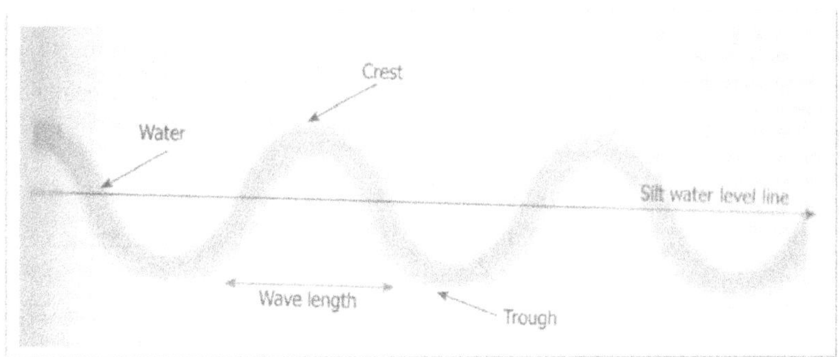

2. Lakes

Lake is a hollow in the earth earth's surface in which water are collected in them. Lakes which are in great size are called *seas* like Caspian Sea, Dead Sea and Aral Sea. Most of lakes are permanent, but some are for temporary.

3. Seas

Sea is an expense of salt water that covers most of the earth's surface. Examples of seas are North Sea, Mediterranean Sea, China Sea, red sea etc.

4. River

River is anybody of fresh water flowing from an upland sources to a large lake or sea fed by springs and tributary streams. River starts on hillsides as a small channels or rills. Some examples of rivers are river Nile, river Amazon, yellow river, and Rufiji River. Rivers have the following parts: *channel* is in which water flows and *flat region or food plain* of valley on either sides of the channel.

Nature of the Ocean Floor

Ocean floor is not smooth in nature but it contains varied reliefs. The relief of the ocean floor is as varied as that of the land surface; it is irregular in shape. There are features on the ocean floor that we do not see because they covered by water. The following are the main features of the ocean floor:

1. *Continental shelf:* Continental shelf is the gentle sloping margin of a continent. The continental shelf is occupied by shallow water that extends from the coast to a depth about 180 to 200m towards the ocean basin. It is excellent for growth of plankton because shallow water allows sun rays to reach its floor.

2. *Continental slope:* Continental slope is the steep slope that extends from the edge of the shelf to the deep sea plain. The continental slope marks the edge of the continent at the beginning of the ocean basin.

3. *Ocean ridge:* Ocean ridge is the raised part of the ocean floor. It takes a form of ridge or plateau on the ocean floor as a sea bed. Mid Atlantic ridge and the Abaltros plateau are examples of ocean ridge which rise above the surface to form oceanic island.

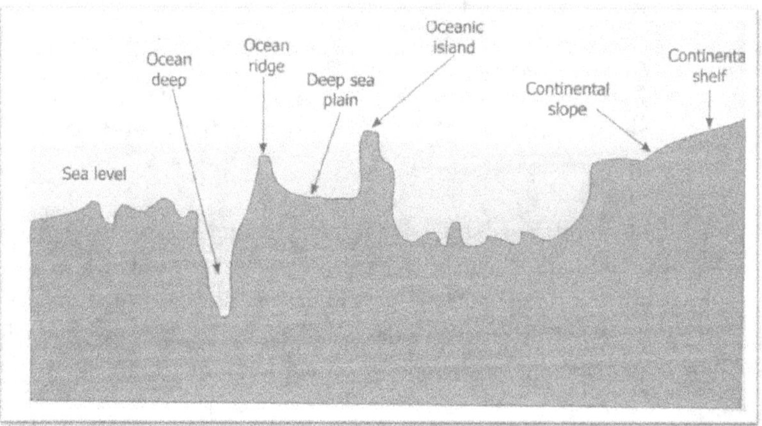

4. *Ocean trenches:* Ocean trenches are long, narrow depressions found on the ocean floors. The deepest known ocean trench is the Marianas Trench near the island of Guam in the Pacific Ocean. It is deepest part is 11911m below sea level.

5. Deep sea plains: Ocean deep sea plain is wide gently sloping surface with a depth of about 300m and 5500m. Deep sea plain is also called *abyssal plain.*

6. Continental islands: Island is a piece of land that is completely surrounded by water. Very small islands are called *islets* or *keys.* The following are three types of islands: *Oceanic islands:* formed due to volcanic activities, *Continental islands:* lies on continental shelf and *Coral islands:* formed from coral rocks.

TRIAL QUESTIONS

1. List down three sources of rivers.

2. Outline two movement of water in the large water bodies.

3. Giving example from each, mention two types of ocean currents.

4. Describe major two relief features of the earth.

5. With the aid of sketch map of East Africa, indicate the largest lakes.

6. Give the meaning of the following terminologies:

    a) Water divide

    b) Catchment area

    c) Underground flow

    d) Drainage

    e) Ocean deep

7. Differentiate between the following:

    a) Fold and block mountain

    b) Tributaries and distributaries

    c) Continental shelf and deep sea plain

    d) Tides and ocean currents

8. Write short notes about:

    a) Tides

b) Waves

c) Volcanic Mountain

d) Valleys

e) Islands.

CHAPTER THREE

THE SOLAR SYSTEM

Our solar system consists of a star of average size and luminosity we call the Sun, the planets (in order of their distance from the Sun) Mercury, Venus, Earth, Mars, Jupiter, Saturn, Uranus, Neptune, and Kuiper Belt objects (e.g., dwarf planets like Pluto), the satellites or moons of the planets, numerous comets, asteroids, meteoroids and the interplanetary medium.

The scientific study of the components of the solar system is called *astronomy*. The study of stars (astronomy) and the movement of planets are used to predict the future, this is called *astrology*.

The Concept of Solar and Solar System

The word "solar" means sun. The Solar System is defined as the arrangement of the planets and solid objects in the space in relation to the position from the Sun. The System is made up of the Sun, Planets, Asteroids, and Meteors, Comets and inter-planetary dust and gases. All the planets and the other bodies revolve around the Sun. The Sun is the central body of the Solar System. All those bodies in Space are held in their positions by the gravitational force of the Sun.

The bodies that revolve around the Sun are kept in their elliptical orbits by the Sun's powerful force of gravity. The sun is the star because it generates its own light like other stars. By definition star is the body that passes and transmits its own light. For the case of planets, in order to remember about planets ascending order from the sun you can use a simple statement as: *My (Mercury)* ***Very (Venus)*** ***Easy (Earth)*** ***Method (Mars)*** ***Just (Jupiter)*** ***Speeds (Saturn)*** ***Up (Uranus)*** ***Naming (Neptune)***.

Components of the Solar System

Solar system has the following main components:

1. The Sun,
2. Planets,
3. Comets,
4. Asteroids,
5. Meteors,
6. Satellites,
7. Stars and
8. Interplanetary dust and gases.

Importance of the Components of Solar System

There are various significances of solar system as some namely in the following:

a) They produce heat and light potential for living organisms for example the sun and moon.
b) They provide habitat for human and other living organisms for example the Earth planet.
c) The falling heavenly objects they tend to form craters which later become attractive sites for tourism industries. For example meteors which produce meteorites that falls on the earth surface and form craters.

About Galaxy

A galaxy is a massive group of stars, star clusters, interstellar gas and dust, and dark matter which is all gravitationally bound together. The word 'galaxy' is derived from the Greek word "galaxias" which means "milky"; it is a reference to our own galaxy the *Milky Way*. There are potentially more than 170 billion galaxies in the observable universe. Some, called dwarf galaxies, are very small with about 10 million stars, while others are huge containing an estimated 100 trillion stars.

Based on shape astronomers have identified various kinds of galaxies including, *elliptical galaxies, spiral galaxies, lenticular galaxies* and *irregular galaxies*. Galaxies often collide with each other. Usually, the stars within each will move past one and other due to the vast space between them. Any gas clouds and dust will interact, forming new stars. Gravity can pull the galaxies into new shapes, two spiral galaxies might join into a new elliptical, others produce bars, rings, or tails. Starburst is a name for galaxies that form a lot of new stars at a fast rate, usually after much molecular cloud is produced as two galaxies merge.

1. Spiral Galaxies

Spiral galaxies are rotating flattened disk-shapes with at least two spiral arms of newer stars extending out from a central bulge of older stars. The dense molecular clouds of hydrogen gas and dust in the spiral arms of spiral galaxies are areas of intense star formation.

Barred spiral galaxies (like our Milky Way) contain a long bar in the middle with spirals arms coming off the ends. Around two-thirds of spiral galaxies contain a barred structure in their center. Barred spiral galaxies have the symbol SB. Spiral galaxies are believed to be younger than elliptical galaxies, as spiral galaxies burn through their gas and dust star formation slows, theylose their spiral shape and slowly evolve into elliptical galaxies.

2. Elliptical Galaxies

Elliptical galaxies are a mass of stars bunched together in the shape of an elliptical disk. Elliptical galaxies are often larger, very old and contain little gas and dust, so therefore form very few new stars. The Hubble classification scheme identifies elliptical galaxies with the letter E, followed by a number representing the degree of ellipticity.

3. Lenticular Galaxies

Lenticular galaxies (S0 symbol) have a bright central bulge with a disk-like structure but, unlike spiral galaxies, the disks have no spiral structure and are not actively forming many stars.

4. Irregular Galaxies

Any galaxy that has no obvious spiral or elliptical structure is called irregular galaxies. Some irregular galaxies would have just formed that way while others are the result of other galaxy types crashing into each other.

Our Milky Way Galaxy

Our Milky Way Galaxy is a barred spiral galaxy about 120, 000 light-years in diameter containing up to 400 billion stars and possibly just as many planets. Our Solar System is located within the disk of the Milky Way Galaxy, around 27,000 light-years from the Galactic Center of the galaxy. Super-massive black holes are believed to sit at the center of most galaxies.

Our Milky Way Galaxy is part of a 'Local Group' of galaxies in which the galaxies move relative to each other. The *Andromeda Galaxy* is the largest galaxy of the local group, followed by the *Milky Way* and the *Triangulum Galaxy*; there are around 30 other smaller galaxies in the group. The largest *galaxies* in the universe may be up to two million light-years long. Sometimes **galaxies** merge with other **galaxies** to form a **galactic** merger.

The Sun and its Characteristics

The Sun is the star of hot gases. It is the star which looks bigger than because it is closer to the earth than other distant stars and also the sun is the large body than other bodies in the solar system. The sun is the source of light and the radiant energy for all heavenly bodies of the solar system. It is the only body in the solar system that generates its own heat and light.

The diameter of the sun is 870, 000 mile or 1, 392, 000km (1.4 Million kilometers). The sun is 109 times larger than the earth and its volume is bigger enough to hold over 1 Million earths. The radius of the sun is approximately to 330, 000 times greater than the earth. The radius of sun is about 700, 000km.

The average distance from the earth to the sun is 9, 300, 000 miles. The sun's temperature is approximately 10, 000 degrees Fahrenheit at the surface and 27, 000, 000 degrees Fahrenheit (5, 500⁰C) at the centre. By its weight, the sun comprises 70% hydrogen, 28% helium, 15% carbon, nitrogen and oxygen and 0.5% all other elements.

Structure of the Sun

The sun is made up with several layers, namely; **1.** *Chromospheres (sphere of color):* is the second outer layer of the sun's atmosphere. **2.** *Corona:* The first outer layer of the sun's atmosphere. **3.** *Core:* is the centre of the sun. **4.** *Photosphere:* The bright surface of the sun. **5.** *Radiation zone* and **6.** *Convection zone.*

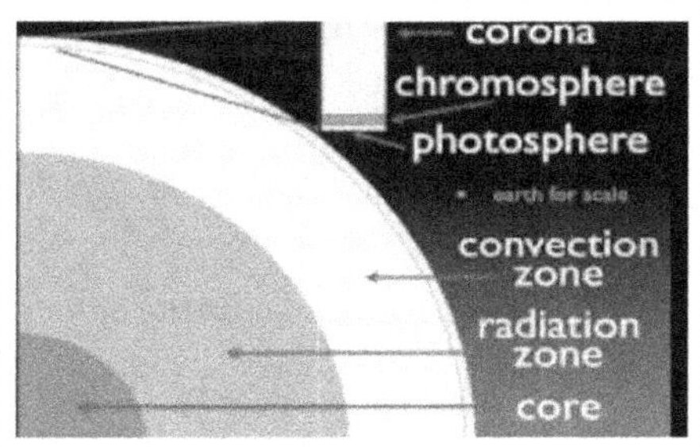

Solar Energy

Energy is the power required to carry out an activity, e.g. to run machine. *Power* is the capacity or ability to do work. Energy is in form of heat, light sound, electrical and chemical energy. *Solar energy* is the heat and light produced from the Sun. the sun provides energy by releasing electromagnetic waves that called sunshine. Solar energy reaches to the earth's surface in form of short waves radiation, visible light and near-ultraviolet light.

The Sun is the source of all energy on the Earth. The energy from the sun flow through living organism starts with sunlight and photosynthesis and then travels through the food chain in which there are primary producers, primary consumers and secondary consumers and decomposers. Solar energy flow is an endless process hence is unexhausted source of energy.

Uses of Solar Energy

Energies provided by the sun have the following different uses:

i.   Drying clothes, meat, fish, fruits and grains.

ii.   Used by growing plants to manufacture their own food through process called photosynthesis.

iii.   Generation of electricity, especially solar panel that convert solar energy to turn into electricity.

iv.   Influences for formation of coal, gas and oil due to the temperature released from the sun. This is through long period buried bodies of plants, animals and other living things to make coal, oil and gases that are formed from dead bodies of organisms.

v.   Contribute much in the formation of clouds and rainfall through evaporation of water caused by the heat of the Sun.

vi.   It is used for giving power to small radios and running small telephone systems by using silicon solar battery.

vii.   Source of vitamin D to human bodies as the bodies absorbs the Sunlight.

viii. Used for domestic purposes like cooking food, heating water etc.

ix.   Source of light during day time and the moon light reflected from sunlight.

Promotion of Environmental Conservation in Using Solar Energy

Solar energy is clean type of energy that suitable for heating and lighting. It does not release fumes or any form of soot. Utilization of Solar energy in manufacturing industries reduces the production of *chlorine* from industrially produced *chloro-floro-carbon gases* which cause depletion of ozone layer. The depletion of the ozone layer causes for global warming, skin cancer and eye problems.

It is used as an alternative source of energy thus reduces depletion of forests for charcoal and firewood uses. The use of solar energy in house hold would reduce the use and demand of wood fuels, and charcoals that pollute and degrade the environment. Solar energy also reduces reliance on fuels, like kerosene and diesel, hence reducing environmental pollution caused by smoke from burning fuels.

Solar Energy and Women Emancipation (a case study from Africa)

In most traditional communities (in villages) in developing countries like Tanzania, rely on wood fuels, for cooking and for other domestic uses. Women and girls tend to walk long distances to the forest or bushes to gather and collect firewood, hence most of the time can be used for gathering firewood unlike to other activities for development and education.

The use of solar power equipment for instance solar cookers and water heaters, would free women and girls from the hard labour of gathering and collecting firewood. This means, the women and girls would then have more time to get involved in schooling and money making activities such as farming and business. This would give women and girls an opportunity to be at the same education, and development levels as men and boys. And this it would also save forest and woodlands from destruction:

Advantages of solar energy

a) It is free; one only has to buy the solar equipment.

b) Maintenance costs for solar equipment are very low.

c) It does not have to be transported because it is available all over the world.

d) It can be captured in every home using solar panel.

e) It does not cause environmental pollution.

f) The solar energy does not get exhausted.

CHAPTER FOUR

THE PLANETS

Planets are bodies that revolve around the Sun. Previously they included Mercury, Venus, Earth, Mars, Jupiter, Saturn, Uranus, Neptune and Pluto. Now, Pluto does not qualify to be among of the planets because it is the smallest and does not revolve around the Sun. There are now officially only eight planets in our Solar System.

The word *Planet* originates from the Greek word *Planetai* which means a *Wandering* as the planets seemed to be moving about in the sky as a *Wandering Stars*. All planets revolve around the sun in the same direction in orbits that are elliptical and nearly in the same plane. The time taken to complete an orbit depends on the distance from the sun. *Orbit* is the path in space which the planet follows as it revolves around the sun.

Conditions for a Heavenly Body to be called a Planet

There some conditions to be fulfilled by the heavenly body so as to be called a planet. The following are some of the conditions:

1) It must have to move around the sun in an orbit.
2) It must be big enough with its own gravitational forces to pull it into the shape of a sphere.
3) It has to have cleared the neighborhood around its orbit of other bodies.

Why Pluto is not among the planet now days?

In August 2006, astronomers from all over the world gathered at the 26th General Assembly of the International Astronomical Union (IAU) in Prague. Among other things, they reorganized our planetary system and agreed on the scientific definition of a planet. Reorganization had become necessary as an increasing number of heavenly bodies were being discovered beyond Pluto's orbits that were about the same size as Pluto.

If these bodies were also granted the status of being planets, this would lead to a real flood of planets in the long term. Under the chair of the well-known female astronomer *Jocelyn Bell*, the astronomers thus agreed on three criteria that a heavenly body must fulfill in order to be a planet. ***First***, the body must orbit the Sun or a star and must not be a star itself. ***Second,*** it must have sufficient mass that is has become spherical due to its own gravity. ***Thirdly***, since its formation, it must have cleared the area around its orbit of small bodies.

Pluto does not satisfy the third criterion - although it fulfills the first two, it was named a *'dwarf planet'* together with *Ceres* and *Eris* (which orbits the Sun outside Neptune's orbit). The updated Solar System now has three categories of planet: the eight classical planets – Mercury to Neptune, a slowly growing number of dwarf planets and the irregularly formed planetoids or Small Solar System Bodies (SSBs).

There are already new mnemonics for remembering the order of the eight planets (moving from the sun), including: "***My Very Elegant Mother Just Served Us Nachos***"; which stands for ***Mercury, Venus, Earth, Mars, Jupiter, Saturn, Uranus*** and ***Neptune.*** Because Pluto is not large enough to "dominate" its orbit, it is not a planet. (Neptune is about 8000 times more massive than Pluto, so Neptune is a planet and Pluto is a dwarf planet).

Other Bodies in the Solar System and their Characteristics:

1. Comets: They are objects with leading heads and bright tails in the sky. In other meaning, comets are ball of rock, ice, dust and frozen gases that orbit the sun. Sometimes they can be seen at night. They are made up with ball ice, dust and the gases; hence these components are referred to as *nucleus of the comets*. They have highly elongated orbits around the Sun. They can be seen from the Earth only when they come close to the Sun. however, hundreds of comets pass through the solar system every year, but very few are noticed from the earth.

2. *Asteroids*: They are solid heavenly bodies revolving around the Sun. they are small planetary bodies in the sky. They are mostly found between the orbits of Mars and Jupiter. They are in thousands and the largest has the diameter of just less than 800 Kilometers. The bodies can only be seen with a telescope because they are very far away. They look like planets and this is why they are called *Planetoids*. Asteroids have highly elliptical orbits and the average taken for one revolve round the sun is about five years.

Some scientists believe that, asteroids are heavenly bodies that failed to form as planets when the solar system was forming, while others believes that, they are piece of planets that broke apart. The largest existing asteroid is called *Cares,* with diameter of about 900kms.

3. *Meteors*: They are pieces of hard matter falling from outer space or, meteors are burning piece of rock in space that forms a bright line across the sky at night falling through the earth's atmosphere. They can be seen when they come close to the earth between 110-145 kilometers whereas as a result of friction with the atmosphere, they become hot and usually disintegrated. They fall on the Earth's surface as large boulders known as *meteorites* or a *meteor* if it is one. These bodies are made of Nickel, Iron and Silica.

They are seen as rapidly moving objects in the sky lasting for a few seconds. The tail light that forms is called a *meteor* or a *shooting star*. If a meteoroid does not completely burn up before it reaches the earth's surface, it is called a *meteorite*. Meteorite may form a large depression on the surface of the earth called *meteor crater.* Examples of the fallen meteorites in Tanzania are at Kimalampaka Kwimba in Mwanza region (1930) and Mbozi district of Mbeya region. In America fallen and found in Arizona.

4. *Natural Satellites:* Natural satellites are the moons of the planets and they can be defined as the small bodies which rotate on their axis and revolve around the planets. There are only seven (7) planets which have satellites apart from 57 to 60 satellites in the Solar System. The number of satellites depends on the size and nature of the planet.

Satellites size range between 10 and 2500km in diameter. The largest known satellite is the earth's moon. Other planets have large moons are Jupiter (Galilean moons), Saturn's moon (Titan) and Neptune's moon (Triton). Something to note, all satellite are opaque bodies like the planets and shine by reflecting sunlight falling on them.

Importance of the Components of the Solar System

1) They produce heat and light potential for living organism. The sun is an example of such components.
2) They produce habitat for human being and other living organism. An example is the planet earth.
3) They form craters (falling meteoroids) which later become attractive for tourism activities.

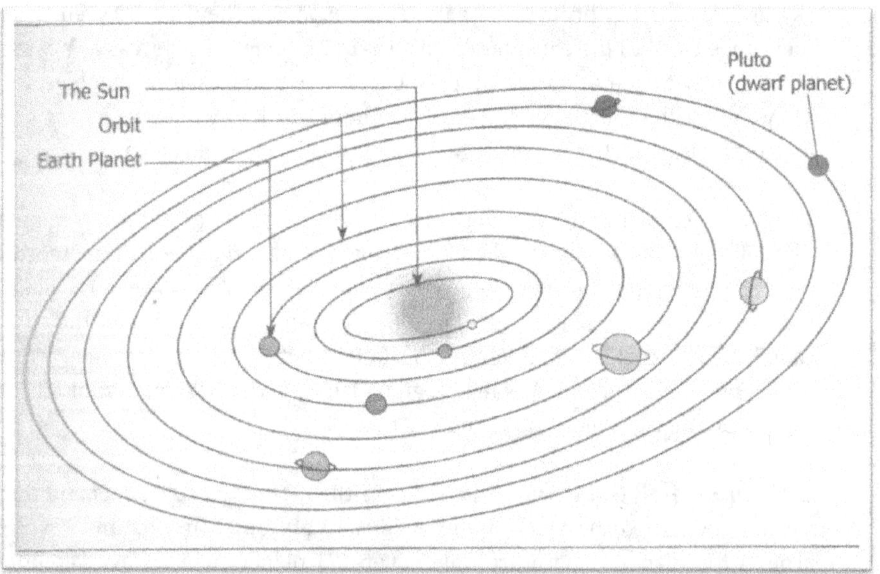

CHAPTER FIVE

THE EARTH PLANET

The earth is the only planet among the planets in the solar system that is known to support life. (Pluto does not qualify any longer to be among the planets because it is the smallest and does not revolve around the sun). Mars and Jupiter are seemed to support life. Water bodies cover about three quarters of the earth's surface. Therefore, the earth is made up of four spheres:

1. The atmosphere (air).
2. The hydrosphere (water bodies).
3. The lithosphere (the solid crust, molten materials) and
4. The biosphere (living organism).

The Shape of the Earth and its Evidence

The shape of the earth is described as spherical but it is not a perfect sphere, it is a flattened sphere, it is slightly wide at the equator and slightly flattened at the north and south poles. This shape is described as *geoid* or *oblate spheroid*. The diameter through the poles is 12,713 kilometers while at the equator it is 12,757 kilometers.

Evidence of the Earth's Shape

There are several evidences which are used to prove that the earth is sphere like and not a flat disc. The following are some of them:

1. Sunrise and Sunset: The earth rotates from West to East, which means that places in the East see the sun before places in the West. If the earth was flat, all places would see the sun at the same time, that is, all places would have sunrise and sunset at the same time.

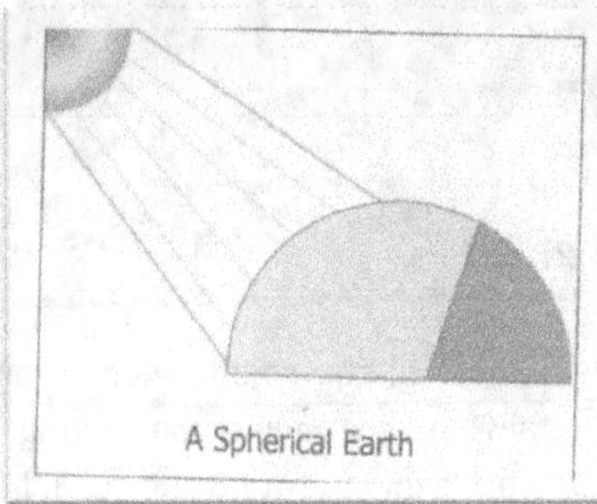

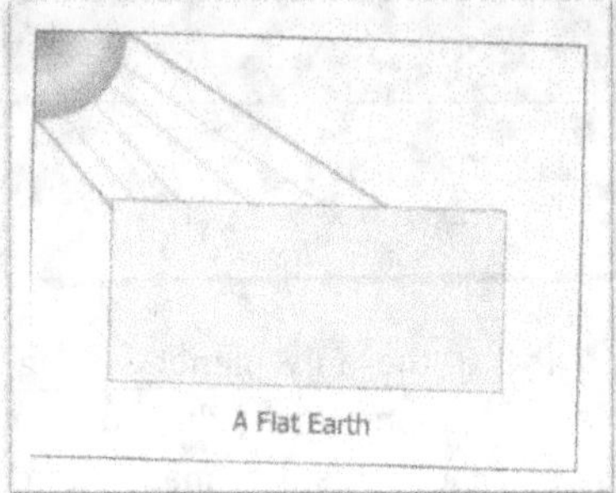

2. Aerial Photographs: Photographs taken by satellites at a great distance above from the earth all show that, the earth's surface is curved and spherical.

3. Circumnavigation of the Earth: If travelling from a certain point of the earth, you will come to the point of origin. The first traveler around the world named Magellan in 1519-1522 proved this. Magellan did not encounter abrupt edge over which he would fall in his voyage.

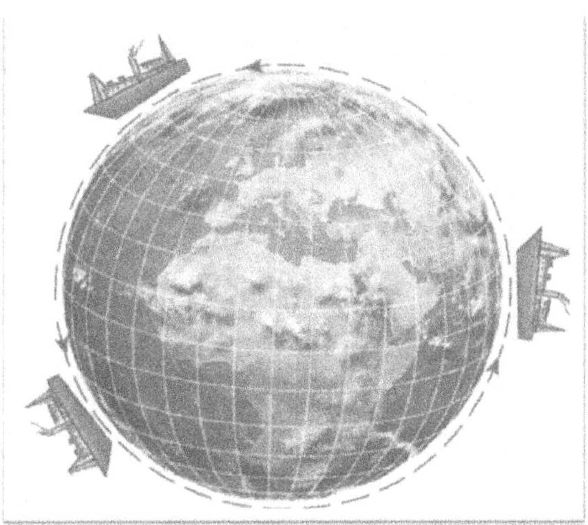

4. *A Ship's Visibility:* as a ship coming towards the land from a distance in the ocean or lake, it does not appear all at once. The ship's smoke and chimney are first seen on the horizon as it comes close to the observer; finally the mast it is fully and clearly seen when the ship come closer near the observer along the shore . This gradual appearance shows that, the ship is sailing over a curved surface. If the earth was flat, a person would be able to see the ship in a sea voyage even a ship is ahead of the person.

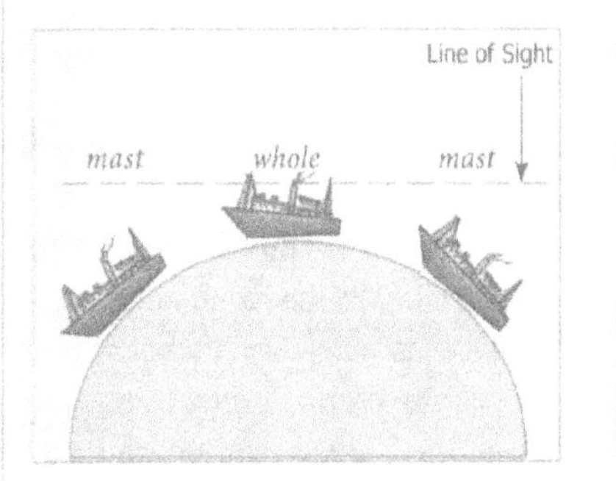

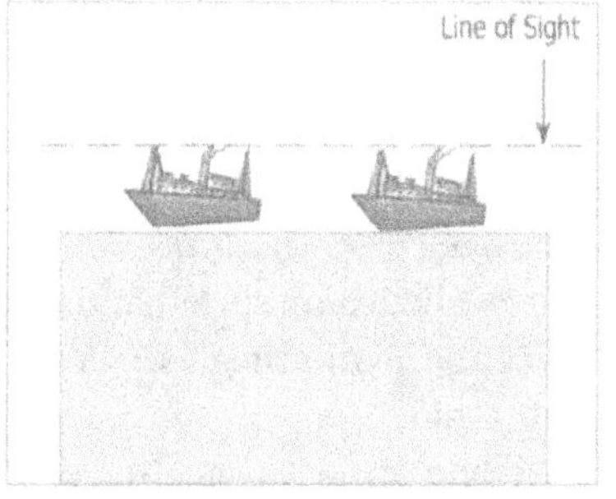

5. Lunar Eclipse: When there is an eclipse of the moon, the shadow of the earth which is thrown on the moon is always rounding. Only a sphere can cast a shadow which is always circular

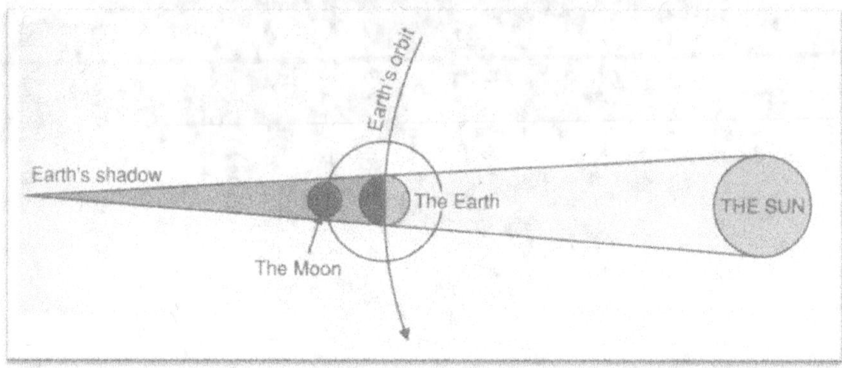

6. The spherical horizon: The limit of the horizon at the place is circular and the horizon widens as the height of the observer increases. When you observe from a very high point, like a very high building, the earth's horizon appears curved or circular.

7. Position of the polar star: The pole star appears vertically overhead at the North Pole. If the earth were flat, the pole star would be overhead at all places on the earth.

8. The observed Bedford experiment: This experiment was conducted many years ago in the Bedford level canal area in Britain. The water level of the canal provided the base of measurement, when three poles were fixed at interval of about 5km such that the poles were rising to the same height above the level of water in canal. When the telescope was placed in such a way that top of the middle pole was in line with that of the two end points. It was found that, the line of sight was intersecting the middle pole that appeared higher owing to the curvature of the earth.

Earth's Movement

The Earth is in motion all the time; people cannot feel this motion because they move with it like all other planets. There are two types of movements of the earth namely:

1. *Rotation*: It is the rotation of the earth on its axis.
2. *Revolution*: It is the revolution of the earth around the sun.

1. Rotation of the Earth

Rotation means spinning of a body on its axis. Rotation of the earth refers to spinning of the earth on its axis. The earth rotates or spins on its axis anti-clockwise direction, from West to East through 360^0 in 24 hours. Thus for every 15 degrees of rotation, the earth take one hour which is the same as four minutes for every one degree.

An axis is an imaginary line joining the North and South poles (North and South) through the center of the Earth. The earth's axis makes an angle of $66^1/_2{}^0$ from the perpendicular.

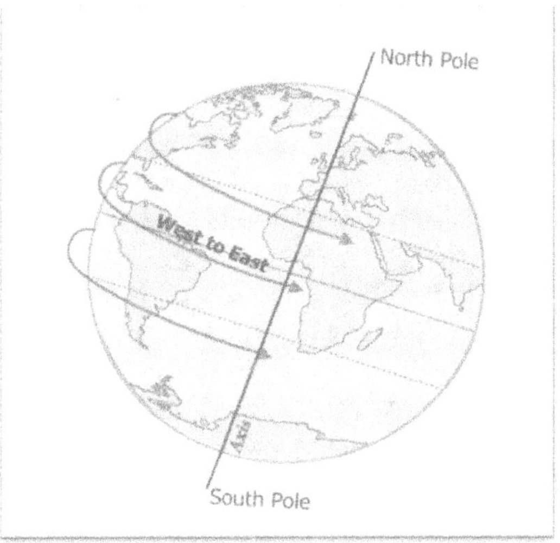

The rotation of the earth is very rapid although it is difficult to feel the motion. At the equator every point of the earth's surface is travelling Eastwards at about 1600 Km per hour. At latitude 40 degrees the speed is about 1280km per hour.

Evidence Proves that the Earth Rotates

1) During the night, stars appear to move across the sky from West to East.
2) If one travels in a fast moving vehicle, will notice trees and other objects on both sides of the road moving fast in the opposite direction.
3) Rising of the sun over the Eastern horizon in the morning. This shows that the point of the observation, that is the south, is moving by rotation from West to East.
4) Occurrence of day and night. During the earth's rotations some regions face the sun while others do not face it. Those regions facing the sun experience day time whereas the regions which are not facing the sun are in darkness (night). This proves that the earth is rotating.
5) Time differences between longitudes.
6) The occurrence of tides in the ocean.

Significances or Effects of the Earth's Rotation

a) *Alternation of day and night:* Rotation of the earth causes the sides of the earth which face the sun to experience daylight which is the day, whereas the side that is not facing the sun at that time will be in darkness (night).

b) *The occurrence of tides:* Tides in the ocean is caused by gravitational forces of the moon and sun upon the rotation of the earth.

c) *Deflection of winds and ocean currents*: This is due to the effects of the earth rotates from west to east hence; winds and ocean tend to deflected.

d) *Time difference between longitudes:* The rotation of the earth is responsible for difference in time between difference places on the earth. It causes the difference of one hour in every 15 degree interval between longitudes. The earth rotates from West to East and takes 24 hours to complete one rotation. The difference in time is 4 minutes for each degree of longitude.

2. Revolution of the Earth

Revolution is defined as the movement of one body round another. Revolution of the earth refers to movement of the earth round the sun. The earth revolves around the sun in an elliptical orbit. Due to the elliptical shape of the earth orbit, the sun is closer to the earth at one point of the year than at another. The farthest (maximum distance) position from the sun in orbit of the earth is called *aphelion* while the nearest position of the earth to the sun is known as *perihelion*.

The Earth is at aphelion each year on 4th July, when it is at the maximum distance of 152 million kilometer form the sun. The earth is at perihelion each year on 3rd January when it is at the minimum distance of 147 million kilometers. The earth's revolution around the sun takes a year (365¼ days) therefore; the speed of revolution is about 29.6 kilometers per second. A normal year has only 365 days.

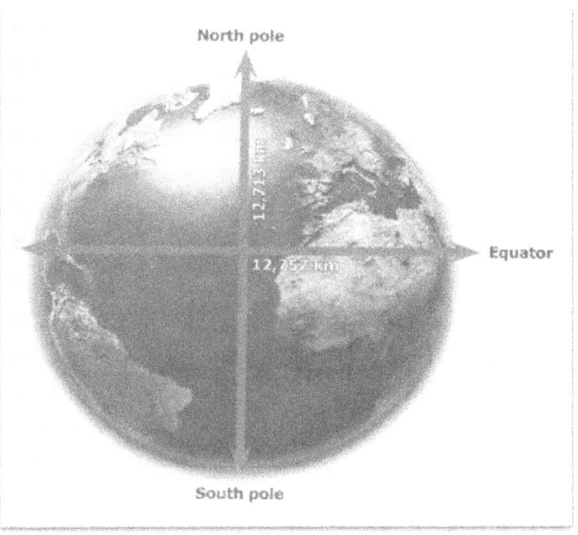

The remaining fraction of ¼ day is added once in four years to make a leap year of 366 days. Every fourth year has 366 days and it is called *leap year.* During leap year, February has 29 days while during non-leap year, February it has 28 days.

Results of the Earth's Revolution around the Sun

The movement of the earth around the sun and the tilting (inclination) of its axis cause the followings:

1. *Change in the position of the midday sun at different times of the year.* As the earth revolves round the sun its position changes and makes it appear as if it is the sun moving.

2. *Varying lengths of day and night at different times of the year.* The axis of the earth is inclined to its elliptical plane at a certain angle of 66.5 degrees. If the axis of the earth were vertical, the sun rays would always be overhead at the Equator, thus all places on the earth would always experiences 12 hours of daylight and 12 hours of night.

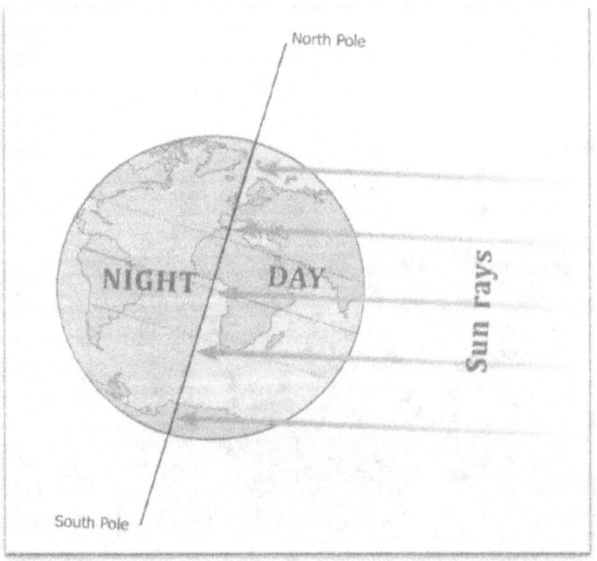

3. *Results the four seasons of the year:* summer, autumn, winter and spring. A Season is one of the distinct period into which the year may be divided. In the northern hemisphere the summer season months are May, June and July. Autumn months are August, September and October, winter months are November, December and January and spring months are February, March and April.

In the Southern hemisphere, summer has November, December and January. Autumn has February, March and April. Winter has May, June and July and spring has August, September and October.

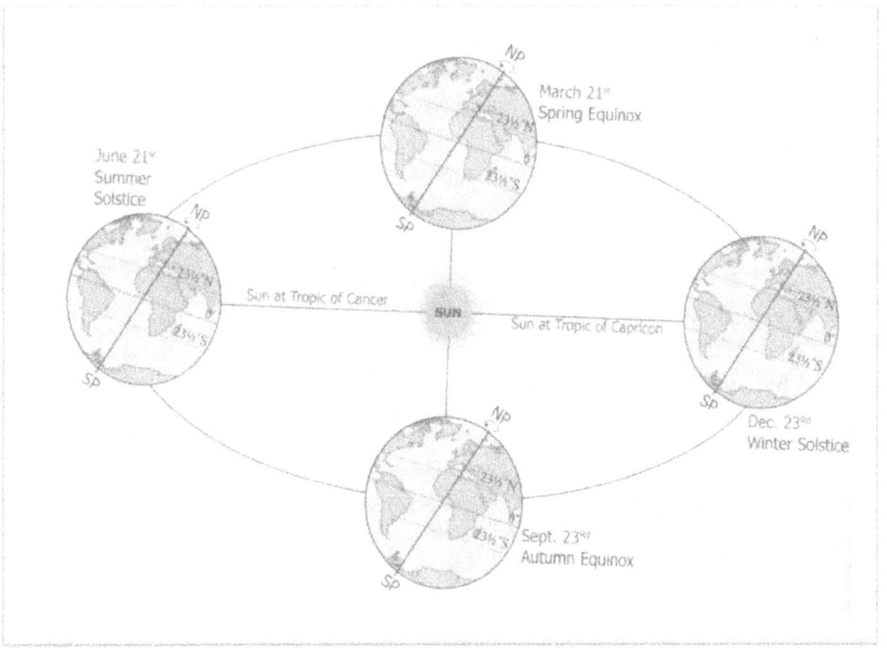

4. *Occurrence of eclipses:* Both solar and lunar eclipses are just caused by the revolution of the earth.

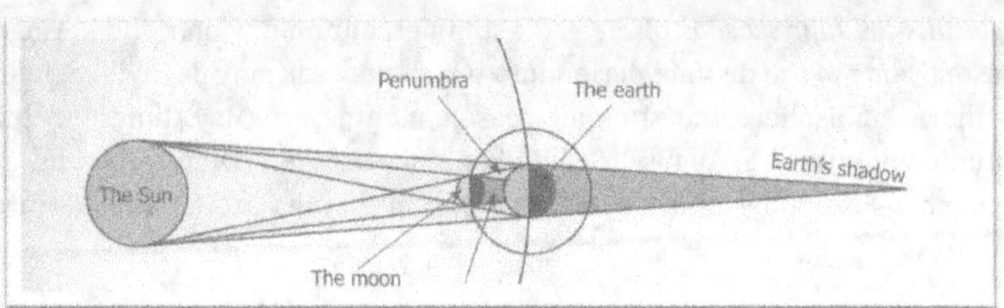

The Moon of the Earth

The moon is a natural satellite of the earth. It has a solid spherical body with a diameter approximately to 3, 480km. The distance from the earth to the moon is 384, 403 kilometers. The moon takes 29 ½ days to make a complete revolution around the earth, in which this period is known as *Lunar Month*. The moon appears to rise in the East and set in the West because the earth spins from West to East. Moon is the nearest heavenly body to the earth just why it appears larger than other heavenly bodies in the sky. The moon rotates on its axis and revolves round the earth.

Eclipses

An eclipse can be defined as at the total or vertical cutting off light received by one celestial or space body from another by interception of third space body in passing between the other two. Simply sometimes eclipse referred as the total or partial blockage of light received by one heavenly body from another. There are two types of eclipses:

    i.   The lunar eclipse
    ii.   The solar eclipse

i.   *The Lunar Eclipse*

This is also known as the eclipse of the moon. It occurs when the earth passes between the moon and the sun thus casting its shadow on the moon. Lunar eclipse happens only on days when there is full moon. There are two shadows in the lunar eclipse:

1) *Umbra*: is the total or complete shadow formed during eclipse. It is the darkness part of the shadow.

2) *Penumbra*: is the part of the shadow which receives only some light during eclipse. It is a partial blockage and therefore a partial shadow. (*See the diagram*).

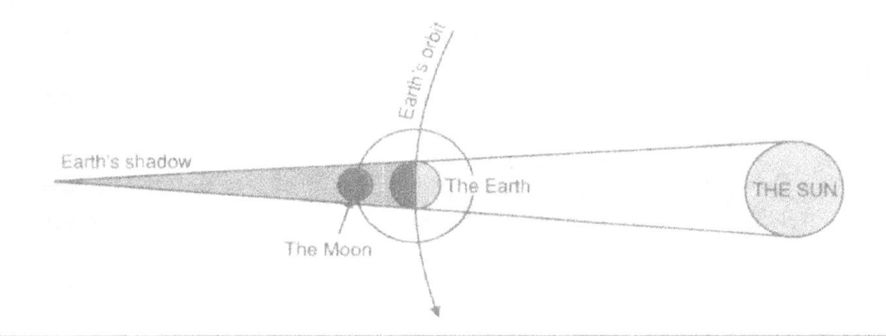

Three Types of Lunar Eclipse:

a) *Penumbral lunar eclipse*: It occurs where the moon passes through the earth's penumbra shadow. This eclipse is very difficult to notice.
b) *Partial lunar eclipse:* It occurs where a portion of moon passes through the earth's umbra shadow. This eclipse is easily to be noticed.
c) *Total lunar eclipse*: This is where the whole moon passes through the earth's umbra shadow.

ii.   *The Solar Eclipse*

This is also known as the eclipse of the sun. It occurs when the moon passes between the earth and the sun, thus casting its shadow over the earth. When viewing a solar eclipse, it is important and advised to wear special eye protection. This is to protect the eye from the harmful rays of the sun that might permanently damage the eyes.

The Apparent Movement of the Overhead Sun

The apparent movement of the overhead sun is related to the different position of the earth on its movement round the sun. The overhead sun appears to move northwards and southwards in a swinging manner. The limit of the overhead sun northwards is 23^0, and people beyond this latitude never see the sun vertically above their heads. The latitude 23^0 North is known as the *Tropical of Cancer* and 23^0 South is known as the *Tropical of Capricorn*.

The places of south of tropic of Capricorn never experience the overhead sun in the year. On 21st June, the sun appears at the tropic of cancer ($23^1/_2{}^0$N). The position of the sun on June 21st is called *Summer Solstice* in the north hemisphere. The apparent movement of the sun concise beyond, the sun is overhead at the tropic of Capricorn $23^1/_2{}^0$S, in which the sun's position is known as *Winter Solstice*, which experienced at the south hemisphere. During the solstice days, the sun appears to stand still between north ward and southwards journey.

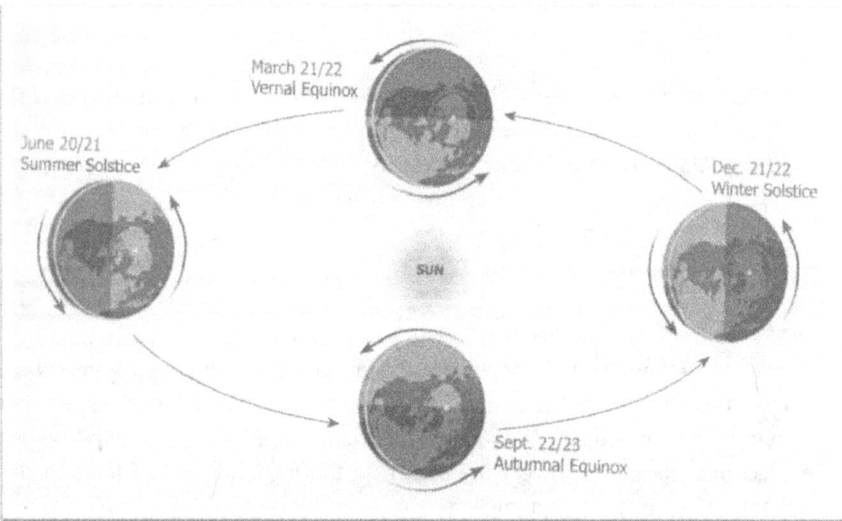

Equinox

Equinox is the period when the sun is overhead at the equator. The sun is overhead at the equator twice a year i.e. 21st March and 23rd September. 21st March referred to *spring equinox*, while 23rd September referred to *autumn equinox*. These two days 21st March and 23rd September; day and night are equal of duration namely 12 hours all places of the earth's surface. Observe the following diagram.

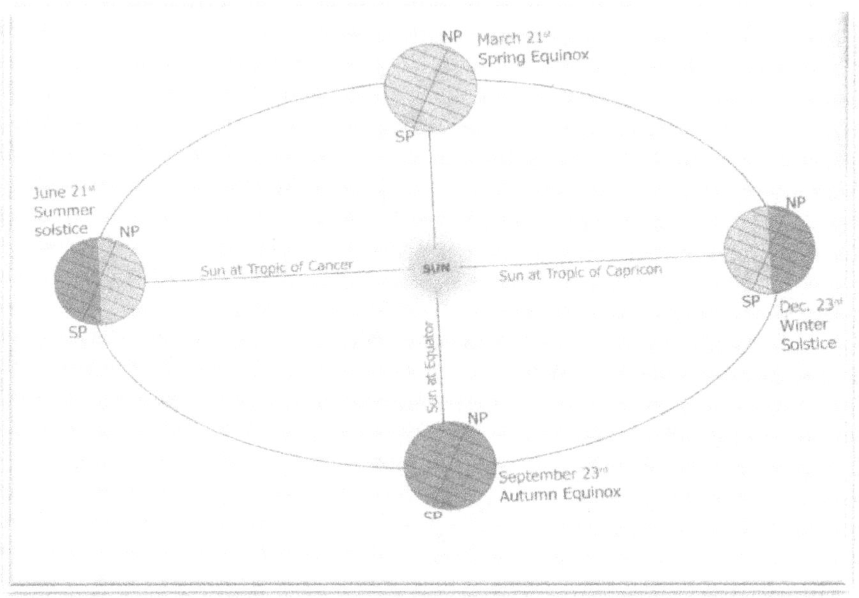

The Parallels and Meridians

Parallel lines are commonly known as *Latitudes*, Meridians are commonly known as *longitudes*. Therefore, parallels and meridians are latitudes and longitudes respectively.

1. Latitudes

Latitude refers to an imaginary line drawn on a map from west to east and forms a circle. In one way or another also latitudes referred to the angular distance North or South of the equator measured in degrees, minutes and seconds. The equator is given a value of 0^0.

Latitudes are numbered from north or south of the equator. These lines do not meet just why are called parallels. Equator is the latitude of an imaginary line which divides the Earth into two hemispheres. The Northern hemisphere has a latitude of 90^0 N and the Southern hemisphere has a latitude of 90^0 S.

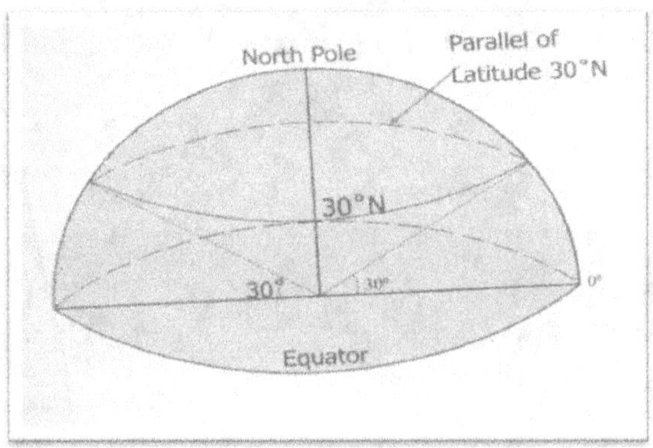

Therefore, Parallels of latitude are particular lines joining all points on the surface of the earth and making an angle of 30^0 N with the equatorial plane. The following are the importance of parallels Include:

a) Equator (0º)
b) Tropic of cancer (23.5 degrees North)
c) Tropic of Capricorn (23.5 degrees South)
d) Arctic Circles (66.5 degrees North)
e) The Antarctic Circle (66.5 degrees South)

2. *Longitudes*

Longitude refers to the angular distance measured in degrees East and West of the Greenwich Meridian or it is an imaginary line drawn on the map from

North Pole to South Pole. The longitude 0^0 is known as Greenwich because it passes through a town in England called Greenwich, it is also known as Prime Meridian because it is the line of reference from which all other meridians are numbered.

All lines of longitude are semi circles of equal length. Lines of longitude are also called meridians. There are 360 degrees in a circle, 180^0 lie east of the Greenwich Meridian and the other 180^0 west of Greenwich. The Greenwich lines have been chosen by convention (meaning that any other lines could have served the same purpose).

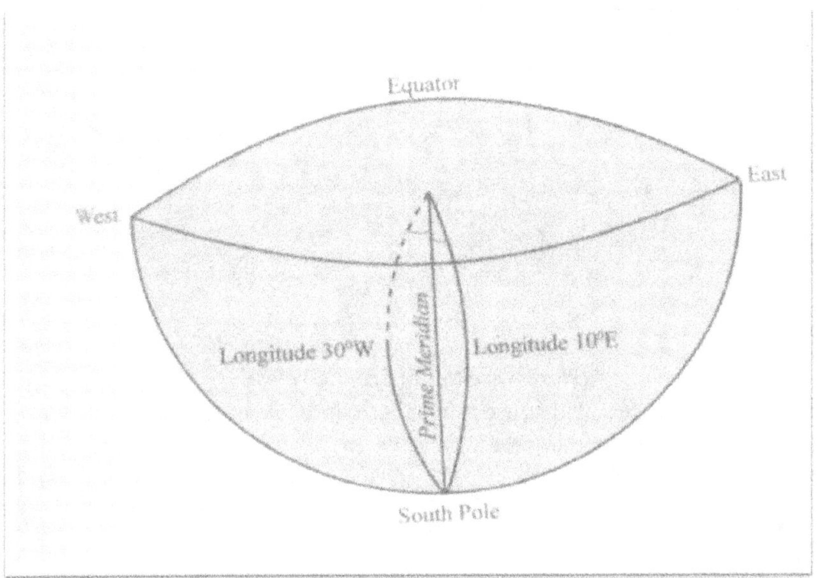

Great Circles

Any circle which divides the globe into hemispheres is a great circle. Great circle is an imaginary circle drawn on the earth. The centre of the circle is the centre of the earth. Among the latitudes, only equator is a great circle while all longitudes are great circle.

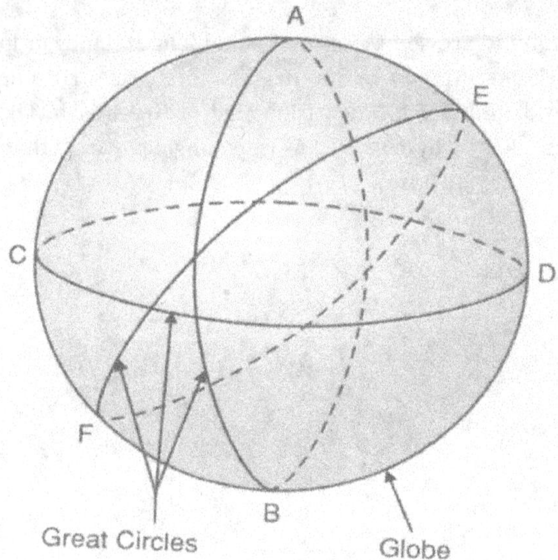

Characteristics of Great Circles:

a) All great circles divide the earth (sphere) into two hemispheres.
b) A great circle is the largest possible circle that can be drawn on the surface of the sphere.
c) The radius of great circles is the same as the radius of the earth.

Important Great Circles:

1. All lines of longitudes (Meridians).
2. Only equator is a great circle among the latitudes.

Uses of Great Circles

Great circles are used to plot routes for ships crossing the vast oceans and aircraft flying great distance in space. Ships and aircrafts travel by following great circles in order to save fuel and time because the shortest route between two places is along the circle of the great circle which passes through them.

Importance of parallels and meridians:

a) They enable to locate places on the maps.
b) Longitudes enable us to calculate local and international time of different places on the earth's surface.
c) Latitudes help us to explain and understand the variations in climate on the surface of the earth.
d) They are both used by pilots and sailors to guide their paths they steers plane or ship.

CHAPTER SIX

LOCAL TIME AND LONGTUDES

The earth rotates on its axis from West to East. Every twenty four hours (one day) the earth takes 360^0 of longitudes to be covered or 1^0 to 4 minutes. Places at a given meridian will experience mid-day at the same time. Time recorded along the same meridian is known as *Local Mean Time* (LMT). The local time at longitude 0^0 is called *Green Meridian Time* (GMT).

The time increases by four (4) minutes for every 1 degree of longitude when one is travelling from West to East. When one is travelling from East to West, the time decreases by four (4) minutes for every one (1) degree of latitudes. ***For example:*** When it is noon (12:00Pm) on the Greenwich meridian (0^0) it will be 2:00 Pm at place 30^0E or 11:00Am at place 15^0West.

(a) Procedure in calculating local time by using longitudes:
a) Note the longitudinal position between the two points.
b) Find the differences in degree of longitude.
c) Multiply this differences by 4 minutes which is the time taken by the earth to rotate through 1^0.
d) Add (for East) or minus (for West).

Worked Example:
1. *What is the local time at Morogoro (Tanzania) 45^0E, when it is noon at Kigali (Rwanda) 30^0E?*

Solution
Different in latitudes or degrees: Kigali 30^0E – Morogoro 45^0E

$$(45^0 - 30^0) = 15^0$$

$$1^0 = 4 \text{minutes}$$

$$15^0 = ?$$
$$15^0 \times 4 \text{ minutes} \div 1^0 = 1\text{hr.}$$

Kigali is noon (which means 12:00 Pm), what will be the time of Morogoro? The time of Morogoro is 12:00 + 1hr = 13: 00 or 1:00 Pm.

The time is added because Morogoro is Eastward from Kigali.

Therefore, the time at Morogoro it will be 1:00 Pm.

(b) Procedures to Calculate the Longitudes of a Place Using Local Time

a) Find the difference in time between two points.
b) Multiply the time by 15^0 or 1^0.
c) Add or minus basing on Eastward or Westward side of the place.

Worked Example:

1. What is the longitude of Dakar Senegal whose local time is 9:00am, when the local time at Accra Ghana is noon?

Solution

Different in time of two points: 12:00 – 9:00 = 3hr

The earth rotate through 15^0 every 1hr: $15^0 \times 3 = 45^0$

The longitude of Accra is 0^0 while the longitude of Dakar is 45^0 (Which is ahead Accra).

Therefore, the Longitude of Dakar is 45^0W.

Other Worked Examples:

1. When the local time of Accra is 2.00pm what will be the local time of Bangui 15^0 East.

Solution

15 degrees - 0 degrees = 15 degrees

15 x 4 minutes = 60

$$\frac{60}{60} = 1 \text{ hour.}$$

Therefore, Accra 2.00 pm + 1.00 hour = 3.00pm

2. When the local times of Nairobi 45 degrees E is 10.00am. Find the Meridian of Kinshasa where the local time is 9.00am.

10.00am Nairobi - 9.00am Kinshasa = 1.00 hour difference

1^0 = 4 minutes

1Hour = 60 minutes (60x1)

$$\frac{60\ minutes}{4\ minutes} = 15 \text{ degrees}$$

45^0E Nairobi -15^0 = 30^0E Kinshasa

Therefore, the longitude or Meridian of Kinshasa is 30 degrees East.

Trial questions:
  1. Supposing the local time at Greenwich meridian (0^0) is noon, what is the local time at Dar es Salaam which is 39^0E?
  2. What is the longitude of a place Y whose local time is 9:00am, when the local time at Greenwich meridian (0^0) is noon?

Time and Time Zone

Time means duration or suitable moment for some purpose or a period that used for an activity. *Time zone* refers to a zone where standard time is accepted throughout a longitudinal zone of 15^0 in width. Each place, nation or country had its own time set according to the mean time. Each time zone has a standard time, which is the time of longitude (meridian) near the centre of time zone.

There is the agreed area to adopt the time by every place from certain meridian, which is known as *standard time.* For example; East African countries agreed to adopt standard time taken from the meridian of 45^0E. However, very large countries like Canada, USA, and Russia have more than one different standard time for different regions within them because they are crossed by many time zones. In Canada, there are about six time zones, USA and Russia about seven time zones.

Essence of Time and Time Zone
a) The importance of time zones is to avoid the problems in telling time if every place had its own time set according to the local mean time.
b) The timetable of various human activities such as television and radio programs would be confusing if they had to show different times.
c) When a whole stretch of land keeps to the same standard time that stretch of land forms a time zone.

Variation of Standard Time in a Single Country
Large countries like USA, China among others have several standard time zones with each time zone covering about 15^0 of longitude. There are 24 times zones in the world. The starting point for dividing the world into 24 times zones is the Greenwich Meridian. The standard time for Greenwich is known as the Greenwich Meridian time (GMT).

International Date Line (I.D.L)
The International Date Line is the line where date is changed or calendar day begins. This line follows approximately the 180^0 Meridian (International Date Line can be seen along the meridian 180^0). 180^0E and 180^0W the time are the same but day are different.

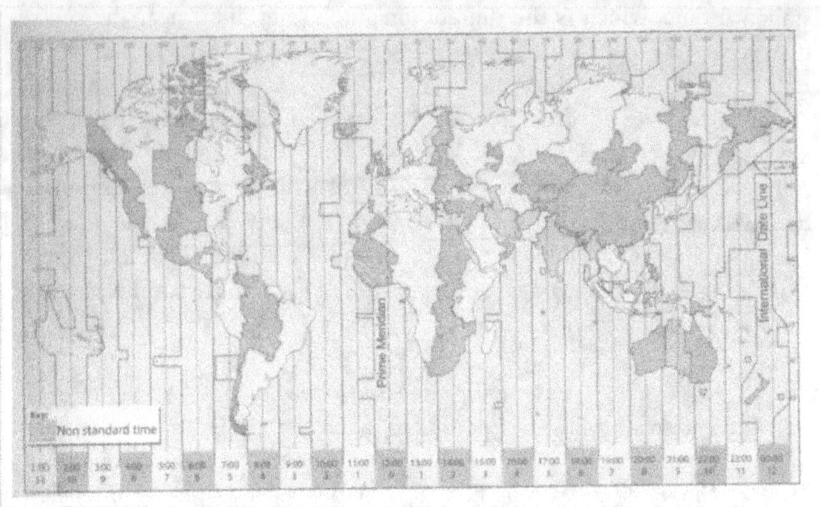

Locating International Date Line

When the time is 6:00pm on Monday 25th December, at Greenwich, the time at 180°E longitudes will be 12 hours ahead of Greenwich Mean Time. The time at 180°W will be 6:00am on Tuesday 26th December. Therefore if one travels eastwards and crosses the date line, one will gain a day whereas one who travels westwards across the line will lose a day.

Lose/Minus	Gain/Minus
West	East
—	+
Lose day	Gain day
Minus	Plus

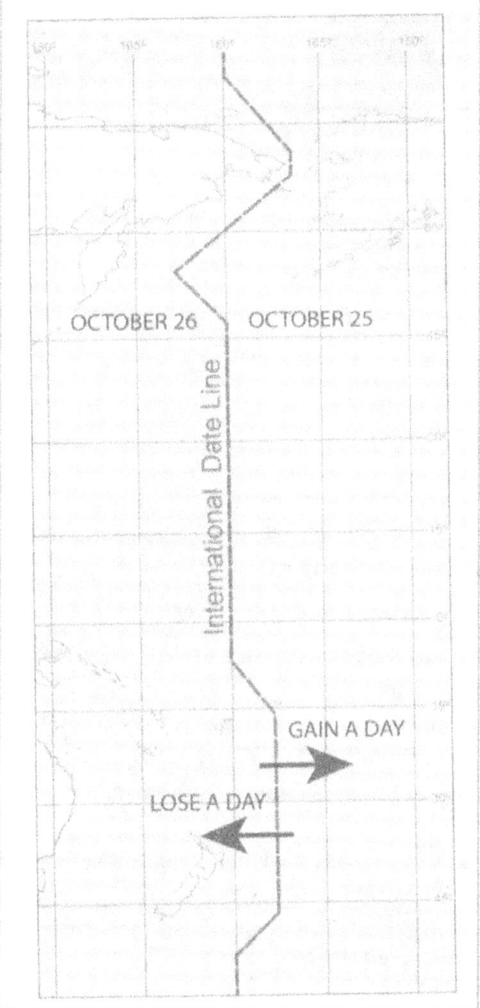
OCTOBER 26
OCTOBER 25
International Date Line
GAIN A DAY
LOSE A DAY

TRIAL QUESTIONS

1. Define the following terms:
   a) Revolution
   b) Rotation
   c) Elliptical orbit
   d) Asteroid
   e) Lunar eclipse
   f) Solar eclipse
   g) Solar system
   h) Planet
   i) Comet
   j) International Date Line

2. What is solar energy?
   a) Describe four uses of solar energy.
   b) Explain the roles of solar energy in environmental conservation.
   c) Explain the roles of solar energy in the emancipation of women.

3. Give six proofs that the earth is spherical.

4. Differentiate between:
   a) Rotation and revolution of the earth.
   b) Axis and orbit of the earth.
   c) Equinox and solstice.

5. (i) Give four effects of the rotation of the earth.

   (ii) State two results of the revolution of the earth.

6. (a) If the local time is noon at Buchanan in Liberia at longitudes 10^0W. What will be the time in Dar es Salaam at longitude 39^0E?

   (b) What is the longitude of place X whose local time is 4:3pm when the local time at longitude 45^0E is 1:00pm?

   (c) If local time at 120^0E is 3:00pm Friday, what is the local time and day at
       (i) Longitude 165^0E

       (ii) Longitude 120^0W

7. (i) Give two dates in the year when the sun's position at noon is over the Tropics of Cancer and Capricorn.

(ii) Why the international date line not straight?

(iii) What is the significance of the International Date Line?

8. Define the following geographical terms:
a) Satellite
b) Season
c) Great circle
d) Longitude
e) Greenwich

BIBLIOGRAPHY

APE NETWORK, (2008). *Ordinary level Geography review*. Dar es Salaam: APE network Publisher.

Buckle C, (1978). *Landforms in Africa*. London: Longman.

Bunnet R. B, (1990). *Physical Geography in Diagrams*. London

Pritchard J. M, (1990). *Practical geography for Africa*. Hong Kong: Longman Group (FE) Ltd.

Pritchard J. M, (1979). *Africa: A study of geography for advanced students*. London: Longman Group Ltd.